INVESTING IN STOCKS

An Essential Investment Guide For Beginners To Learn The
Basics Of Trading In The Stock Market

MARK KRATTER

content within this book has been derived from various sources. Please consult a licensed professional before attempting any techniques outlined in this book.

By reading this document, the reader agrees that under no circumstances is the author responsible for any losses, direct or indirect, which are incurred as a result of the use of information contained within this document, including, but not limited to, errors, omissions, or inaccuracies.

Table of Contents

Introduction

When you learned to drive, you didn't just jump in the car and turn it on. Instead, someone walked you through exactly what to do before you started the car. You were told what the stick-shift or automatic PRNDL (Park-Reverse-Neutral-Drive-Low) was for. You were told how to move the mirrors, what was forward and reverse, and other buttons in the car. Before you invest in the stock market, you need to walk, not run. You need a guide that tells you how things work, so you avoid making costly mistakes. As long as you know how something works, you don't have to be afraid of the reality of it. Many people do not understand investing, so the stock market scares them. The reality is—you just need to know how it works, the parts that make it work, and you can set up an investment strategy that works.

A stock is usually referred to as a share. It is a share in a company that is looking for investors. These investors provide capital for the company to grow the company. When a company first offers shares, it is called an IPO or Initial Public Offering. The share price is set on the estimated worth of the company, as well as the number of shares available for sale.

For the shares to be publicly offered, a company needs to be listed on a stock exchange, like the NYSE (New York Stock Exchange).

Traders and investors can then buy and sell stocks, but the company will only make money with the IPO. After the IPO is over, it is simply businessmen, individuals, and investors trading the stocks between themselves to make a profit and dividends.

Buying Shares on the Stock Market

Investors and traders sell stocks after the IPO based on the perceived value. A company's value can go up or down, which is where investors make their money. A company's stock price that rises can provide a profit. If an investor has purchased those shares and the price or company value decreases, then the investor will lose money. It is also the investors and traders that will push the price in an up or down direction.

Investors have one of two goals: investing in the short or the long term. A long-term investment is based on a stock continuing to rise in price. A short-term investment is to gain quick cash and pulling out before the stock price decreases.

Mature companies offer dividends to their shareholders. If you have stocks, then you are a shareholder in a company. If you hold the stocks long enough and have enough stock in a company, you can vote on new board members. Dividends are company profits that you get a cut of.

Investors will make money on the price fluctuations and dividends. A seller is often trying to gain a profit by selling to a new buyer.

The new buyer is also trying to buy-in as low as possible, so that when the stock price continues to increase, they will make a profit.

The profit is calculated by taking the initial buy-in price and subtracting it from the closing or sale price. For example, if you buy into Google at $400 and wait for it to go up to $600, then the profit is $200 per share.

Sellers can push the price down due to supply and demand. This financial market works based on supply and demand.

Supply and Demand Concept

You should already know that in economics, when there is an oversupply of a product, the price is low. There is no demand for the product; therefore, a company or, in this case, a stock is not of interest.

When there is an undersupply of something like a stock, the demand is high. With more interested parties, a price will continue to increase.

If there is an even amount of supply and demand, then equality exists, and there is no movement to see.

For the stock market, when too many people sell a stock, the price will decline. When too many people buy a stock, the price will continue to rise. If there is an equal number of shares and interests, then the price usually trades sideways because there is a balance.

As you learn about the stock market, you will hear the word volume, often. Volume is the number of shares that change hands on a daily basis. Millions of shares can be traded on the stock exchange in a day as investors attempt to make money from increasing or decreasing prices.

The stock market works based on the interest or volume of traders. If a stock does not have any volume or very little, then it is not being actively traded; thus the price is not moving. Traders such as market makers get into the market in order to buy or sell stocks for companies with low volume. They do not stop a stock from rising or falling. Instead, market makers just try to garner interest in the company's stock.

What Most People Do

When it comes to the stock market and traders, most individuals are looking for the high-volume trades, with fluctuating prices. They get in, make a profit, and get out to find the next big profit.

Final Thoughts

The shares are first released from a company to gain investment funds. The shares are then traded as a way to garner dividends and profit from the up and downtrends in the market. The market also allows you to invest in various exchanges around the world, as long as your broker provides access. Most people trade in their country's stock market or the largest in their region like the Japan Stock Exchange, London Stock Exchange, and NYSE.

Swing trading is popular amongst many investors. It can be applied to a wide array of financial instruments including currencies, futures, stocks, and options. Each of these instruments has its own advantages and disadvantages. It is the only style that utilizes both long-term as well as day trading strategies.

Chapter 1 - How to Become a Successful Day Trader?

To be a successful day trader, you must have a goal in mind before investing.

Setting a Goal

Define what makes you want to get up and go to work every day. Want to go on vacation? Need to pay off student loans? Want a new car? Whatever the reason may be, defining a goal will help new traders be able to reach their potential.

A goal should always be measurable and have a timeframe attached to it. Measurable goals can help people see how far they have come, and timeframes allow for meeting deadlines and defining new goals.

An important thing to remember is that day trading is not a "get-rich-quick" scheme. Keeping goals realistic will help bring success.

Strategies

The next step after defining your goal is to strategize on how it's going to become a reality.

It is important to know some concepts that directly relate to your strategy. These concepts are the required capital and leverage.

Leverage

Day traders use either their own money (cash account) or by borrowing money from a broker (margin account).

This is an important decision to make. Trading with a cash account is often a safer option, but profits are limited to the amount of cash the trader has available.

Margin accounts are the most popular among day traders. With a margin account, traders can use the money provided by the broker to increase earnings per transaction, but they will also be increasing the amount they lose if the market turns for the worse.

Brokers also may ask for a deposit into the account before allowing a trader to use the platform.

Leverage is a straightforward concept with stocks. Let us say a trader buys $1000 of XYZ Inc. by putting up $500 and borrowing the other half of the money from the broker. The ending value after the trade is $1040. This would mean that the net equity will be $540, and the trader will have gotten an 8% return on the investment when the change in stock price was only 4%. So, the leverage allowed the trader to double his returns. However, this could have ultimately been double the loss as well.

How Much Should You Risk Per Trade?

In stock trading, a lot usually has 100 shares, and price increments are very small. Suppose a trader buys a lot at $20 per share and places the stop-loss at $19.50. In this case, the risk will be $0.50. For 100 shares, the total amount at risk will be $50.

Is this a suitable trade to make? Most traders recommend staying at or below the 1% mark as an accepted risk. Regardless of how good of an opportunity, a trader should keep 99% of the account balance intact.

Let us apply this logic to the above example. We are risking a total of $50 and our total account balance is $2000. By dividing $2000 by 1%, we get how much balance our account should have. The division gives us $20, which is 2.5x more than the amount of risk $50. So, the risk involved in making this trade is significantly higher than what we should risk per trade.

16

As per the risk strategy, to perform this trade, we need to have not less than $5000 in the account balance (which translates to $50 risk tolerance).

Stock Selection

Successful day traders always choose to trade stocks with the highest liquidity (traded at high volumes). One of the best things about choosing a liquid stock is that it can be easily bought and sold. This is since it has a large volume of shares that you can trade without having to worry about significant price changes.

In day trading, day traders must apply speed and precision in their strategies. Working with a high-volume stock will make it easier for day traders to enter and exit trades.

Day traders also need to consider the depth of the market (how many shares are available to trade). This will tell them how many shares they can buy from a certain corporation without causing significant price appreciation.

Day traders also choose stocks with medium to high volatility. Price movement is very important for day traders because this is where they can make money. Thus, choosing volatile stocks is important. Volatile stocks are those companies that are experiencing large price swings, resulting in a significant gap in their Intraday high points and low points.

Day trader chooses stocks that are group followers. What are group followers? Basically, these are stocks or equities that imitate the movements of their specific sector or index groups. How do you find these stocks? Simple. Just observe all those individual stock prices that increase when the index or sector goes upward.

Take note that if your strategy is trading the same stock every day, you do not have to mind if your stock is a group follower. The wisest thing you can do is to just focus your attention on that one stock.

Only pay attention to the current Intraday trend. If you have been around with other traders, you might have been given wise advice to "trade with the trend." The most experienced traders will advise to "trade with the trend because "the trend is the day trader best friend."

But of course, as a trader, you also have to accept that there is also an end to the trend… and when that time comes, you do have to part ways. But as long as the trend is there, you have to ride the waves. How do you do it? Well, keep it simple.

If you see that there is an uptrend, take long positions. As we said earlier, trends will not be there to stay, but you can make around one or two trades before the trend changes. If you are lucky, you can even make more.

But remember, once the dominant trend changes, go out and do not come back again till a new trend can be observed.

If you want to pick out the best stocks for Intraday trading, try to compare them with the S&P 500 or Nasdaq indexes. Ideally, look for stocks that have moderate to high correlation with these indexes. Now, what kind of stocks should you be trading during an uptrend?

The Entry Strategy

Always wait for the pullback, sometimes, traders become too impatient, especially during an upward trend that they decide to go on another route. But this should not be if you want to gain the best profits. Experts say that waiting for a pullback will give you lots of benefits. How will you go about this?

Start by looking at the trend lines so that you will have a rough estimate of where the price waves start and stop. You can use this when you are choosing stocks for trading to see if you can make an entry into the next price wave early on that will take you in the direction of the trend. If you are planning to buy a stock that you are expected to rise in value, buy it after you note a downward movement in the price and moves towards the higher point.

Always take profits regularly. As a trader, you do not really have a lot of time to capture profits, which is why it is very important that you do not spend a lot of time in trades that are not letting you make money. Also, make sure to avoid getting into trades that are not moving in the right direction.

When can you make profits? When the market is moving in an upward direction, you can take profits when the price matches or goes slightly above the price high in the current trend.

Stop-loss

Stop-loss is your safeguard. It is the stock price level, which, if reached, you will ask your broker to automatically exit the trade and sell the stocks you bought. This helps to limit your losses.

The determination of the level of the stop-loss is based on your risk tolerance and the technical analysis of the trend.

An important thing to understand here is the relation between your entry point and stop-loss. The stop-loss is not static, but once you enter the trade you can change your stop-loss, according to the behavior of the tread, but remember you must only change the stop-loss in the up direction, never set it below the level you specified when you chose your entry point.

The Exit Strategy

If there is an entry point to trading, there is also an exit point. If you have been trading for a while, you will know that entering a trade is quite easier than getting out of it. Exiting a trade is the part where you will know if you made a profit or you acquired losses.

The easiest way to close or exit a trade is to use a profit target. According to Investopedia, a profit target is a "predetermined point at which an investor will exit a trade in a profitable position." Say, for example, your profit target is $11.35. You bought the stock at $11.25 and sold it at $11.35. When the price reaches $11.35, you can go ahead and exit the trade.

Now, you have to take note that placing a profit target also needs to be balanced. Your main goal here is to earn the optimum profit potential, according to the market tendencies that you are trading in. If you get too greedy and put a high price, you might not reach your target. If you put it too close, you might not earn a lot of profit for your efforts. So, it is up to you to decide, based on your skills

21

as a trader. One of the pros of using profit targets is that you already know the risks and rewards of the trade before you even place a trade.

Another positive aspect is that if you base your profit target on the objective analysis, it will help you avoid feeling different emotions in trading such as availability bias, loss aversion, and lottery syndrome. This is because you already know that your profit target is in a good place since it is based on the actual chart that is being analyzed.

One of the downsides of using profit targets is that it requires a lot of skills. You cannot put them randomly based on gut feeling. So, if you think you are not that skilled enough on this strategy, try to think of other ways, or better yet, make yourself more skillful.

Another downside is that there is always a possibility that your profit target will not be reached. This is not good because if you continue to place your profit targets too far, you will not be winning any trades. In the same way, if your profit target is placed too close, you will not earn any profit from taking risks.

Thankfully, there are a few methods in which you can may the most out of your profit targets.

Chapter 2 - Picking the Best Time to Trade

Whether you are a beginner trader or a professional, you need to start relying on consistency. This is going to make it easier for you to pick the right stocks to invest in and can help you figure out if you are going to make a profit or not. For example, a stock that has consistent ups and downs in the market will be much easier to invest in because you know when the high and the low points will occur. A stock that is really volatile and doesn't have a pattern at all can be hard to invest in because you never know where it will go from one day to the next. There are a few tips that you can follow to make picking the best time to trade an easier decision.

When you want to trade in stocks, the best time to do this is the first two hours after your chosen market has opened, and then in the last hours before closing. So, trading between 9:30 and 11:30 is a good time to begin. This time is very volatile, which can give you a lot of price changes and a lot of potentials to make profits. Then, you can also consider trading at three to four in the afternoon because some big movements can occur at these times as well. For traders who can't spend all day trading and who only have a few hours available, the morning session is the best option.

If you are looking to trade in futures, when the market opens is the best time to trade. Active futures have trading activity all of the

24

time, so the best opportunities for this will often start earlier than when the stock market opens. Try to focus your energy on trading between 8:30 to 11:00. The official time for closing the futures market can vary, but you can also look at trading during the last hour as well.

During the week, the forex market is available for trading all day long. The most popular day trading pair that you may want to work with is EUR/USD. The time when the forex market is the most volatile is between six and five GMT. For a day trader who wants to work with the forex market, you should focus most of your energy on trading during that time. Often, the biggest changes in prices will occur from 12 PM to 3 PM GMT. This is when both the US and the London markets are open, which means that both groups are doing a lot of trading at the same time.

Despite the common belief about day trading, you don't have to spend all day on the computer doing your trades, unless you want to. This can be hard to keep up with and may end up leading you to a lot of anxiety and stress. Chances are, many traders are going to be more consistent and make more profits if you only spend a few hours trading in the market each day. Going with some of the times that we have listed above, depending on the market you want to trade in, can make a big difference.

Overall, you can earn a profit when you trade any time of the day as long as you have a good trading strategy and you know when to enter and when to exit the market. So, if there is some reason why you can't be available right at the beginning or right at the end of the market, then don't fret about it too much. You can always trade at the time that works best for you.

Chapter 3 - Options Trading

Options trading is not new to the game of finance. In fact, the practice has been around since before 332 BC, as its first record was mentioned in a book called Politics, published in 332 BC by Aristotle. This practice allowed people to purchase the right to buy an asset without actually buying the asset outright.

Aristotle introduced this topic by writing about a man called Thales of Miletus. Thales was a revered astronomer, philosopher, and mathematician in ancient Greece. His practice of options trading started when he used the stars and weather patterns to predict that a huge olive harvest would come in the following year. With the first prediction, he then stated that olive presses would be in high demand to facilitate such a huge harvest. Forward-thinker that he was, Thales understood that he could turn a huge profit if he was the one to own all of the olive presses in the region.

While he did not have the kind of money that allowed him to buy all of the olive presses outright, he did use the small amount that he did have to secure the use of all olive presses in that region by using the olive presses themselves as the underlying asset to facilitate the transaction.

His prediction came true and the olive harvest was plentiful. As the one who had the option to all the olive presses in the region, Thales had the option to use them himself during harvest time (exercising the option) or sell them to other people who would pay more for the same right that he owned at the time (selling the options to earn a profit). He chose to sell the right to use the olive presses to harvesters and thus, turned a huge profit.

Options trading found its way into modern trading practices as it moved into European classic economics and finance in 1636. Due to unregulated practices, options trading got a bad reputation. However, this did not stop investors from acknowledging that trading options allowed them to gain powerful leverage in the finance arena.

Options trading was brought into the United States in 1872 by an American financier called Russell Sage. By using options trading, Sage was able to accumulate millions of dollars in just a few years, even though the practice of trading options was illiquid and unstandardized during that time. He even bought a seat in the NYSE in 1874. Unfortunately, Sage lost a small fortune during the stock market crash of 1884 and gave up trading options. Other traders and investors saw the potential that options trading had, though, and continued the practice.

It took about 100 years, but options trading became standardized and regulated by the government as it gained increasing popularity, and more advances were made in defining how the public traded options. I am ever grateful that the practice stood the test of time and became an integral part of modern stock marketing investing.

My start on the stock market came with options trading. Options trading allowed me to enter the stock market back when I did not have the finances to buy and sell stock outright. Even though the learning curb was sharp, especially since information was not as readily available back when I just started, the benefits allowed me to accumulate enough wealth so that I could turn to investing in pricier forms of trading on the stock market like buying and selling stocks, mutual funds and exchange-traded funds.

Even though the affordability was great, it was the no obligation nature of this form of trading that pulled me in the hardest back then. By utilizing options trading, I was under no legal commitment to buy or sell anything unless it was advantageous for me to do so. As a man who did not have as many assets signed to his name back when I just started as a trader, this was great because the risks were significantly lower compared to the act of outright buying and selling of stocks.

Because of the powerful leverage trading options allows me, I still use this trading practice today as a way to keep my portfolio balanced and to enter markets, I am unsure about but want to test for profitability. The best part is that getting started with options trading is not all that different than getting started with buying and selling stocks. Ensure that this practice is incorporated into your trading plan, that you have the necessary accounts and representation through a brokerage firm, get your feet wet with paper trading and then choose your trading style, then you will be all set to start trading options! Day trading is the full-time practice of stock market trading and positions trading. It is the stock market trading style most commonly used by professionals. It is also the style most used for options trading.

What are Options?

Stocks and options are two items that are often mistakenly thought to be the same, but they are not the same thing. Stocks are a typical component of options. Options are a great way of investing in the stock market without outright buying stock or any other security. This method of investing allows investors to invest in the stock market with a lower amount while still having the potential to earn the same profit that a stocks trader would.

Options are financial contracts that derived their value from the securities attached to them. The contract states that the holder of the option has the right (option) to buy or sell the security on or by a date specified at a specific price. This specified date is called the expiration date. The name option comes from the fact that there is no obligation for the holder of the contract to take any particular course of action.

The options that the option holder has include:

- Sell the option to another investor.
- Exercise the contract and buy the asset.
- Exercise the option and sell all or part of the asset.
- Allow the option to expire without following any particular course of action.

The specific selling or buying price that the option can be exercised for is called the strike price. This price does not change, no matter what happens after the date of signing.

Instead of buying or selling the security, investors of options pay a premium to the seller of the option. Options premium pricing is a complex process because there are so many factors that go into developing each one. It would be a simple process if the premium was just based on the value of the stock or other securities, but it is not. And there is not going around the process either because premium pricing needs to be fair to all the parties involved in the transaction.

The intrinsic value of the security also factors into the development of the option premium. This value is determined by finding the difference between the current market price of the security and the strike price of the option.

The time value is also another factor that makes up the premium of an option. Time value is the amount an investor would willingly pay in addition to the premium because there is the underlying belief that the security value will rise in the future.

Other factors that affect the creation of options premium include:

- Volatility
- Interest rates
- Dividends

Luckily, there are pricing models that help with the creation of option premiums so it does not have to be calculated manually.

Chapter 4 - Position Trading

Position trading is when you hang on to a stock for several weeks or even months. Position traders hang on for a longer period than swing traders. You are more focused on a longer-term game plan and you're confident that the gains that you would accomplish with such a longer timeline are going to be higher than if you tried other strategies. The biggest factors for position trading involve three elements: news trends, earnings cycle, and industry trends.

News Trends

Traders who use a position trading strategy essentially invest in the stock. The fact that they're digging in for up to several months shows that they're investing in the value of the stock being appreciated by the broader market.

One of the main factors that they base this strategy on is the news involving the particular stock. Maybe there's some sort of drug application approval that's spending. Maybe there's some sort of a new patent or program that was launched. Whatever the case may be, there is an event that was made known to the public, and there is some sort of a cut off in the future regarding a decision on that event.

For example, a biotechnology company may have been developing a breakthrough cancer drug for several years. All that time, the

35

stock may have been going up and down or trading sideways. A position trader would take a position on that stock if there was news that within a few weeks or a few months, there would be an FDA decision regarding its drug application.

Now, what makes many biotechnology stocks fairly good position plays is the fact that they are fairly predictable in terms of their news cycles. In the United States, for new medication to be approved by the FDA, there have to be some several phases in the drug application. There are the lab trials, the clinical trials, and the formal application. Each of these news events can be points in time where the position trader can buy into the company.

Using the biotechnology example once again, if a company is working on an anti-cancer drug, they would first announce that their lab results indicate that they have a promising compound. When the news comes out, this can be a buying opportunity. However, it's anybody's guess whether this seemingly promising technology would really pan out, as far as commercialization is concerned, because the drug still has to go from internal laboratory testing to wider lab testing, to human clinical trials, and then formal application.

A position trader can take a position on the stock and wait until the next phase comes. Usually, they would wait until that point in time where clinical trials look so promising that the company can then file a formal application. The stock can move quite a bit once a formal application is tendered by the company.

Can you imagine the effect on the stock when the FDA finally approves the application? So, the key point here is there are fairly well-defined milestones for a biotechnology company's proposed drug to get approved. Position traders can look at the milestones and take positions accordingly. It's not uncommon for traders who specialize in biotechnology stocks to enter and leave a biotech stock several times as the company moves closer and closer to drug approval.

Other news trends to look out for involve strategic partnerships. For example, a company has just partnered with a large retail or pharmaceutical chain spread throughout the United States. Such deals and business developments can have a very positive material impact on a company's sales figures.

The position trader would then look at the announcement and then buy into the company based on the projected timeline of when the results of that static partnership will be released. Depending on how big the deal is, the position trader can actually make quite a bit of money if the distribution deal of the business alliance has a fairly significant impact on the company's bottom line.

Earnings Cycle

Another fairly predictable milestone or series of events position traders take advantage of our earnings cycles. When a company is about to announce its earnings in a month, a position trader would look at recent news releases to see if there is a positive trend here, or if there is a negative trend. Either way, the position trader would take up a position.

In the case of a positive trend, the position trader would buy long. In terms of negative trends, the trader would sell short. Whatever the case may be, there is a fairly short and predictable period of time between the time the trader took up a position and when the earnings event comes. Either the company made more money or made less money, the event will come, and the position trader can then liquidate his or her position.

It's important to note that there's a little bit of complication. Wall Street has evolved to the point that if a company manages to meet expectations, that may not be enough in of itself to boost the company's stock. In many cases, Wall Street expects companies to beat street expectations to gain a nice boost up.

For example, if Facebook announced that they are going to be making a dollar share and Facebook comes in at exactly a dollar share, chances are that performance was already factored into the stock price of Facebook by the time its next earnings cycle milestone comes up.

Now, compare this with Facebook announcing that it made a $1.25 profit per share. Assuming that the consensus expectation was $1 per share, this makes for tremendous news. A position trader that bought before the earnings cycle stands to gain a lot of money due to the fact that the company beat expectations. Always factor in the power of street expectations when it comes to the earnings cycle.

Don't be surprised if you take a long position several weeks before the earnings cycle plays out, and only for your stock to remain the same price or to even decline. Pay attention to street expectations. It is not uncommon for stocks to hit their announced earnings target and still see their stock price sink. Why? Wall Street was expecting the company to beat expectations. Simply coming in to meet expectations is not enough.

If you think that's bad, it's especially worse if the company misses expectations. If, for example, Amazon stock was expected to earn a dollar per share, but the actual figure is 90 cents per share, this can put a tremendous downward pressure on the stock. Always factor in expectations.

Industry Trends

Another big factor in position trading involves industry trends. If you noticed that an industry, as a whole, is poised for a breakout, then you can take a position in leading companies in that industry. It all depends on whether this industry breakout or recovery is factored into the prices of the stock price of the biggest companies in that industry.

The key to playing industry trends is not to buy the giant players in that industry. Chances are whatever appreciation you get would be quite incremental because everybody's paying attention to those companies. A lot of people are playing those companies. Whatever upward movement in your positions may be would basically be diluted by the huge number of people buying and selling that stock.

Instead, look for mid-tier companies that have a track record of appreciating quite well during industry recoveries. Alternatively, you can take positions in growth stocks within that industry. The reason why you should pursue this strategy is that the weight of return to your position would probably be much higher compared to you betting on the biggest players in that industry you're tracking.

You have to understand the biggest players in any industry are usually already bought into by big mutual funds and pension funds. In short, their institutional coverage is very high, so they really have to outperform the industry tremendously for their stocks to get a nice lift up. This is not the case with middle tier or up and coming companies within that industry. These companies' stock prices can benefit tremendously if there is any sort of positive industry trend.

Risks in Position Trading

The biggest risk that you undertake when doing position trading doesn't involve your stock going down. Okay, let's just get that out of the way. Even if your stock were to tank, you should have a stop limit order on your stocks. Meaning, you decide for yourself going in what is the most you can afford to lose. You then put a stop limit sell order on that price.

For example, you buy into a stock that's worth $20. You then arrive at 10% as the maximum you're willing to lose on that position. Accordingly, if the stock ever dips down to $18, you will automatically neutralize your position. You will liquidate. You are completely out of the stock. This is how you protect yourself from your long position going south.

Believe me, this happens quite a bit. It doesn't happen all the time, but it does happen, so you need to protect yourself. At least you only lost at least 10%. You can then play the market again to recover. Also, keep in mind that when you lose money in stock trades, you can use that loss as an offset regarding any gains in the future. Still, the biggest worry you'll have when using a position trading strategy to stocks is that the stocks really don't go anywhere.

41

If you think about it, it may actually even be a good thing if the stock just sinks. Because once it sinks, you have set up your stop-limit order so that you are out of that stock. It just didn't pan out. The worst thing that can happen is for the stock to essentially track sideways. For example, if you buy a company that is worth $20 share and for the whole year, you took a position and the price of the company basically went from $20 to $19 to $21, and never really varied. Why is this a problem?

Well, the problem here is your money is not growing so you're not beating inflation. Second, you're paying a huge amount of money in the form of opportunity costs. Can you imagine if you were to have not invested in that stock in the first place and traded another stock that is volatile enough for you to lock in a sizable profit? Which position would you rather be in?

You better believe that the opportunity cost in position trading can be quite huge. This is why a lot of position traders diversify their long positions. They know that out of a basket of stocks, some would sink so they would immediately liquidate their position.

Always pay attention to the turnover of your capital because the timeframe might be so long that it turns out that it was really not worth your time and energy to have gotten into that stock at all. While the stock might appreciate a couple of percentage here and there, you're looking for a fairly substantial return to fully recoup and make up for whatever opportunity costs you suffered.

This is the key to position trading. Make sure that the gain you got compensates or more than compensates for the amount of time you waited for the stock to appreciate.

Chapter 5 - Scalping

Traders can be divided into three types: swing traders, day traders, and scalpers. The three methods can be integrated, which is my preferred mode of operation.

Scalping refers to very short-term trades. Swing traders hold stocks over to the next day, and day traders generally try to get as much from the stock as possible within one day of trading. Both swing and day traders generally base their systems on technical analysis with a touch of fundamental analysis.

Scalpers are based one hundred percent on technical analysis. Their goal is the very short term. Changes of just a few cents for several seconds up to some minutes are sufficient. This means that in order to earn a livelihood from the market, scalpers need to trade in relatively larger amounts than day or swing traders. Scalpers with little backing (which is, sadly, the case for most of them) make up for what their pocket lacks by trading in financial products, which can be leveraged more than the typical leverage of the world of stock trading. These may include futures, leveraged twenty times more, options, and of course, FOREX (foreign exchange), which can reach leveraging of up to 500 times more, expressed as 500:1 margin. The absurdity is that trading in these strongly-leveraged products is harder and incredibly riskier than stock trading.

Nonetheless, the dream of "striking it rich quick" draws people with no funds and no experience into the hardest areas of trading, where they will often begin, and almost invariably end, their trading careers.

Scalping Techniques

The first condition: you need to keep your finger on the mouse, and your eyes glued to the screen. You need to give your full attention to the stock. You must buy and sell with precise LIMIT orders.

You must absolutely NOT chase the stock, because, with scalping, profit or loss is measured in just a few cents. In many cases, I place an exit order in advance.

For example: if I buy 3000 shares at $20 and anticipate an increase of 30 cents, I will set a sell limit order in my trading platform of:

- 1000 shares at 20.15

- 1000 shares at 20.25

- And wait with my finger on the mouse for the first sign of weakness in order to sell the remaining 1000 shares

Smart Money

Scalps are meant to be short term and are therefore not executed in small quantities. Trading in small quantities of shares causes the "small-money syndrome" and leads to failure.

Scalping is not executed in small quantities of shares. New traders scalping in small quantities, such as 300 shares, find themselves caught in the trap of negligible profits, or as the phenomenon is known, the "small-money syndrome." Selling 100 shares for a profit of 15 cents seems like too small a yield, so they will try to drag the trade out for a few more cents, and usually discover that they have waited too long before selling. The stock pulls back down by 10 cents, so it does not pay to sell because the profit is even less now, and they wait a bit longer. Then the stock returns to their entry point, or even below it, and the scalping ends in a loss!

With large quantities of shares, by contrast, a decent profit is earned with each partial trade locked in, without the need to cope with the small-money syndrome.

The One-Cent Scalp

Cent scalping is a trading method geared at making profits of one or just a few cents, from light intraday fluctuations in stocks with "locked prices." Stocks with locked prices are stocks in which hundreds, if not thousands of traders, are operating, executing bids and asks at one cent above or below the stock's traded price. This is not a classic trading method based on noticeable intraday fluctuations resulting from breakouts, breakdowns, or direction changes. In contrast with everything we have learned so far, scalping for one cent is based chiefly on lack of volatility.

One Cent Scalping and the Commission Barrier

The first condition for participating in this method is to have a large trading account. If you want to profit from the movement of one cent and still overcome the barrier of commission, you need to operate with no less than 10,000 shares. A profit of one cent on 10,000 shares is worth $100, from which commission must still be deducted. The commissions with this method are the key to success or failure.

Here is an example: let us say that you profited one cent on 10,000 shares, producing $100. Let's assume that you pay a commission of one cent per share, and you bought 10,000 shares. That totals $100 profit, canceled out by the commission, and when you sell, that costs another $100. Altogether, a loss of $100. Even if you paid commission of one-tenth of a cent, totaling $20 for both buy and sell executions, you have still left 20% of your profit with the broker.

This may sound reasonable to you, but you must also take into account the sad fact that when you lose (at least 30% of your executions will end up as losses), the loss plus the commission will total $120. The weighted average is definitely to your detriment.

The solution: unlike the method of charging one cent per share, which will only be worthwhile if you operate in quantities of up to 2000 shares per click, when you trade in large fixed amounts, you need to ask your broker to define a different commission system based on the Per Trade Commission Plan rather than the Per Share Commission Plan. If you trade in large amounts, it is probable that you will be able to close on a price of $3 to $6 per click of the button, unlimited in quantity.

Large-scale traders usually receive commissions rather than pay them. How? When you set your bid and ask orders and wait for their execution, you are adding liquidity to the market! When you do that, as we have already learned, you receive a commission of $2 per 1000 shares from the ECN. With a simple calculation, you can understand that the relatively small quantity of 10,000 shares will bring you an ECN return of 0.2 cents per share, which is $20, while you paid only $6. What would happen with a quantity of 100,000 shares? The ECN return is worth $200, while the commission you pay is still $6. Can you see where this is going? I am familiar with traders who make their living from buying and selling a share at exactly the same price, for profits of hundreds of dollars from the ECN return alone. If they're lucky, they also manage to earn another cent per share.

Sound easy? No, it isn't easy at all!

One-Cent Scalping: The Method First find a low-priced stock

This should ideally be in the $5 to $10 range, with low volatility and a volume of tens of millions of shares per day.

The candidates change during different periods of market activity, volatility, and price. Remember that volatility is this method's worst enemy. Just imagine how much you could lose if the stock moved ten cents against you! This is also why you MUST operate according to the following rules:

1. The stock must be moving sideways with no trend, or in industry terms, the stock must have a locked price.

2. The stock must show no volatility and movement of up to 5-10 cents per day

3. The market is moving sideways with no trend (generally occurs during lunch hours)

4. The stock is priced up to $10. You can buy cheap stocks in large quantities even if your name is not Warren Buffet

5. The stock shows large trading volume of tens of millions per day

The simplest way to choose a stock is to fish it out of the list that always contains the "top ten" high volume stocks traded on

NASDAQ or NYSE. Notice that I do not relate to stocks that made it into the list by chance, but those who are on that listing constantly. On some days, you might choose Bank of America (BAC) or Intel (INTC), Microsoft (MSFT) or others. Citigroup (C) used to be the scalpers' favorite as long as its price hovered around the $4 mark in volumes of hundreds of millions of shares per day before the reverse split was executed, as already described.

When you bring these stocks up on your screen, you will see intraday volumes of tens, if not hundreds of millions of shares, and enormous numbers of bidders and askers. Many of them are playing the one-cent game.

Who, in fact, shifts the stock if no one wants it to move more than one cent? Of course, this would not be the scalpers working at the single cent level, because they are basically locking the price and preventing movement. The real change comes from the public and from funds bidding and asking with long-term investment in mind, and they are not interested in whether the stock has gone up or down one-cent.

Let's assume you have chosen your stock and it's time to trade. The operation itself is fairly simple but requires a good deal of experience. First, even if the price is moving sideways, examine the overall market trend and the stock's trend. If the trend is up, you will want to execute a long rather than a short, and vice versa. Now you need to enter your buy limit order in the BID, and wait patiently until sellers hit your bid. The moment you have bought the desired quantity, you enter a sell limit order on the ASK side, with a profit target of 1 to 3 cents, and wait for buyers to hit your ask in the reverse direction.

Notice that there is no need to use the short order since for most of the trading platforms, the regular SELL will operate exactly like a short. Now that you have sold the quantity you bought at a profit, and added to that sale a double quantity, you are in a short and therefore need to position a double quantity on the BID side with a targeted profit of 1 to 3 cents, repeating the cycle. Once the market becomes more volatile, and based on the premise that you are on the right side of market direction, you need to cancel the exit order and try to profit from a few more cents beyond the original profit target.

I wish to stress, yet again, that this method sounds simple. In reality, it requires a great deal of patience, self-discipline, and deep familiarity with the market. You need to follow the stock chart in one-minute candles. You also need to watch the market chart, which will indicate if you need to flee the trade with an unexpected loss, or cancel an exit order and let the market take you to unanticipated profits of a few additional cents.

Chapter 6 - Value Investing

Value investing or fundamental investing is also known as the Warren Buffett School of Investing. Warren Buffett is a world-famous investor. He lives in Omaha, Nebraska, and this man is responsible for growing his investors' money several thousand times. I'm not saying that his stocks are worth several thousand dollars, I'm talking several thousand percent appreciations. That's how awesome of an investor Warren Buffet is.

The interesting thing about his investing style is he really doesn't pay attention to what the current price of the company is. Instead, he looks at long term value. It may well turn out that the stock of a company seems fairly high by today's standards. However, to Buffett, the stock is actually cheap in light of its future value.

The secret to value investing is the future value. You basically would have to look at the track record of the company, its current operations and health, as well as the health of the industry it's in. You then project this information in the future factoring in potential future conditions. Once you have a fairly clear picture, you then buy in, and it's important to note that you basically don't leave. That's the whole point of value investing.

You buy and you hold. You're playing the long game. This strategy is strictly for people who buy long. You might be asking yourself, well, if I buy long then I might be suffering opportunity cost because I could have been making more money in the short term buying a more volatile stock?

Believe me, if you play the biotech or internet stocks, they can be quite volatile. It's not uncommon for traders to make thousands of dollars every single day of volatility of these stocks. They move that quickly. Warren Buffett doesn't care about any of that. Instead, his game is to basically hold the company for several years or even decades and at the end of that long period, the stock has split many times or has gone up in value so much.

If you ever need proof of this, look at his main investment vehicle, Berkshire Hathaway. Can you imagine if you have bought Berkshire Hathaway in the 80s? You would be a millionaire many times over today. That's how awesome of an investor Warren Buffet is. He's all about the long game. He's all about patient investing.

Now, value investing may not fit your investment goals. If your immediate goal is to have your money appreciate by 10% or 15% per year, value investing may not be a slam dunk. You have to understand that value investing looks at growth over time. It may be substantial growth. We're talking about the company's stock price doubling or even tripling, but it's anybody's guess when this will exactly happen.

It's not uncommon for a stock to only appreciate 5% the next year, and then the year after that goes up to 20%, and then dips down to 10%, so on and so forth. But when you average everything out, it turns out that the stock has actually doubled, tripled, or even quadrupled in price.

How to do Value Investing

Warren Buffett is known for simply reading the financial statements of a company, as well as their financial papers in the comfort of his office. He would then make phone calls to make million-dollar stock purchases. That's all he does. He usually never goes to the actual company. He usually never reads the paper or checks out the news regarding the company.

All he pays attention to are their numbers. I don't expect you to master the game so well that you only need to see numbers. This is why you need to pay attention to the following factors.

Focus on CASH FLOW

Solid companies have cash flow volumes that justify their price. The company must be generating revenue. Even if it is no earning a profit, it must have enough cash flow to justify its price either now or at some point in the future. Depending on how speculative the stock is, cash flow is determined by either P/E or price-to-book.

(P/E) Price to Earnings Ratio: The company's earnings per share is cross-referenced to its current stock price. For example: if a company is earning $1 per share is trading at $20 per share, its P/E ratio is 20. This is an indication of cash flow value in reference to its current price. If you're going to use P/E as your cash flow factor, you should compare different stocks that have the same fundamentals (industry positioning, book value, growth factors, and others).

Price to book Ratio: After reading a company's balance sheet, you will be aware of all the assets a company has. After proper depreciation and discounting, whatever amount left is the liquidation value of the company's assets. In other words, if you were going to liquidate the company and get cash for all assets and you take out whatever debt the company owes, what's left is its book value. Price to book is the ratio of how many times the company's book value is multiplied to produce its current per share value. For example: if you have a company that has a book value of $10 per share and it trades for $100 per share, the price to book value is 10.

Please note that there are many other cash flow-based value calculation methods, but P/E and price to book are the most common and are enough to guide any beginner investor. As you become more proficient at trading, you might want to scale up using other methods at calculating cash flow.

Focus on Industry Leaders

The first thing you need to do is to look for industry leaders or potential leaders in an industry. It's important to look at solid companies. These companies are doing something right. They're making money. They have made an impact. They've got their act together. It's important to focus on these qualities.

The problem with a lot of stock out there is that a lot of them are sold based on hype and potential. For example, Twitter traded as high as the low 40s because people are optimistic that somehow, someway, it's going to make money. Its valuation wasn't really based on how the company was run, how much money it was making, its position in the industry. None of that matter. All the focus was on potential growth.

Not so with value investing. You look at the actual position of the company and the fact that it is already making money. You start with that fact. The company has to be already well-positioned. This doesn't mean that the company has already dominated its industry or is the number one player. It can be an up and comer. What's important is that it has the house in order.

It must have Solid Financials

A key indicator that a company has its financial house in order is that it has zero to low debt. A company that has almost no debt and a low stock price is actually quite underpriced. This is the kind of combination that Warren Buffett gets excited about. He knows that chances are quite good that for some reason or another, the market simply is not acknowledging the solid fundamentals of a company. And one key factor in that is its debt exposure.

If the company has almost zero debt and a low stock price and a solid market or industry presence, then the company has a good chance of being a good value investment. However, you need to look at other factors as well.

The Company is in a Growing Industry

Now, can you imagine doing your research in stocks and finding a company that is a soon to be an industry leader, or is already an industry leader and has zero debt? It is also very profitable currently. On top of all of this, its stock is fairly low, as measured by price per earnings ratio (P/E). Sounds like a slam dunk, right?

Well, hold your horses. Pay attention to the company that industry is in. It may well turn out that that company is the only gem in that industry because that industry is basically going downhill. In that situation, that company is probably going to have a bleak future. Its stock price might look good now, but it's only a matter of time until that company implodes or has to reinvent itself and enter another industry.

Pay attention to the industry. Is it under a tremendous amount of disruption? Or is it still a growing industry? The problem with industries that are under a tremendous amount of disruption is that you really don't know the direction the industry would go.

For example, the Eastman Kodak Corporation was the top dog of the photographic materials industry. Thanks to the rise of digital cameras, the photographic material industry is a shadow of its former self. It still exists in a very limited form, but it's definitely not big enough to sustain a company that's as gigantic as the Eastman Kodak.

Do you see how this works? And the problem was that the industry that was under serious disruption during the 90s and early 2000s. Steer clear from companies that are under disruption because it's anybody's guess what the ultimate direction of the technology or business strategies of the companies in that industry.

Heavy Cash Flow and large Cash Position

Another factor value investor looks at is how much cash a company has on its book. Now, this is the key indicator of how well that company is run. If a company is profitable but it essentially just burns up its remaining cash on research and development, the company might not be a solid value investment because it's essentially spending a lot of money to make a lot of money.

Ultimately, it's basically just trying to tread water. This is not always the case. It also depends on the industry. Still, if you notice that a company has a lot of cash in its balance sheet and almost zero debt, that company is doing something right and if you can see that the cash at hand is growing over time, then this is a key indicator that this company may be a solid value investment, with everything else being equal.

Pay attention to accounts receivable. While a healthy level of accounts receivables is fine, a company that has an extremely high A/R level merits further and deeper analysis. It might be having a tough time collecting and you need to be very careful about how they log these. The company might only seem like it is worth a lot of money.

"Underappreciated Stocks"

Warren Buffett makes a big deal about underappreciated stocks. In fact, in many of his interviews, he talks about buying stocks that are underappreciated. Now, a lot of people would define "underappreciated stocks" as companies whose stock prices are a bargain compared to other companies in the Dow Jones Industrial Average.

This is a misconception. A stock is underappreciated, in classical value investment terms, not based on how it compares to other companies but based on its potential future value.

Chapter 7 - Dividend Investing

What is Dividend Investing?

Dividend Investing is a term describing an approach in investment, which entails purchasing stocks that have dividends. The main goal of Dividend investing is the generation of a stable passive income. Dividend investing is not as simple as its definition. There are intricacies involved.

For those that are not in the finance field, this may make the reading of the book a little bit difficult to understand. However, here are some terms you should look out for in the course of reading. Knowing these terms should help simply their use as we move forward.

Stock: This term refers to a kind of security that equates proportionate ownership in the issuer company. Alternatively, a stock is called shares.

Dividend: This term is simply the portion of a company's profit paid to its shareholders. Dividends are not necessarily cash. They are in shares and other properties.

If you are not well convinced about dividend investing, it is time you stopped doubting the potentials of this investment strategy. There are many benefits of dividend investing, but the accessible advantage that everyone will derive from is that it is an ideal source of retirement income. When you retire, you have the privilege to take some of your dividend payments and still retain ownership of stocks, which will continually pay you for the rest of your life.

Why Invest in Dividend Stocks?

Notwithstanding the economic importance of dividend stocks, there are articles, books, and even experts' comments that discredit Dividend investing. As a result, many people are left undecided about the decision to invest in dividend stocks. "What if the company slashes the price of their dividends abruptly?"

"I read it up an article that the payment of dividends does not determine shares prices." These comments are some of the reasons why specific individuals are left undecided about the decision to invest in dividend stocks. Undoubtedly, nothing in this world has no pros and cons. The same principle applies to investment in dividend stocks. The good news about investing in dividend stocks is that the advantages greatly outweigh the cons.

Besides, the few drawbacks of investing in dividend stocks should not make you lose a chance of a steady income. As an investor, if you want to make it financially, you must be willing to take a risk. Even if you choose not to invest in a dividend stock, there is a risk in your decision. You risk the chance of not benefiting from the earnings of dividend stocks.

Despite the few limitations of dividend stocks, there are countless reasons why you should invest in dividend stocks. So, to the big question:

What Are the Benefits of Investing in Dividend Stocks?

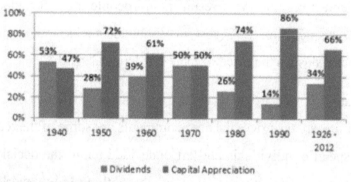

Components of Monthly Total Return on S&P 500

■ Dividends ■ Capital Appreciation

Source: Dow Jones S&P Indices LLC

Image showing the rate at which dividend investing can multiply your returns over time.

Dividend Stocks Investment Is an Avenue to Secure a Stable Stream of Income

One merit of dividend stock over other types of stocks is that it helps you achieve a source of passive income that is both steady and reliable. Unlike other forms of investments, you don't have to sell anything to make a profit.

When you invest in other types of stocks, you tend not to make a profit until you sell them. The set back of this characteristic is that you merely have a paper profit until you sell something. Yes, you make a profit. But the gain is only on paper as you are unable to cash out your rewards and earnings till you sell something. So, most investments are not ideal for a steady passive income.

The situation is different when you invest in dividend stocks. The primary thing that distinct dividend stocks from other investment options are that there are no paper profits. When you invest in Dividend investing, you have the assurance of cashing out raw and cold cash. There is no strict requirement to tell your broker to sell something when you are involved in Dividend investing.

Dividends are your earned money. Once paid, they cannot withdraw from you; this is the best part about investing in dividend stocks.

Also, the norm is that companies pay dividends frequently of a fiscal quarter (that is, every three months). If you are an investor seeking to multiply his/her income; dividend stocks, this is an investment option that you should consider. There is a guarantee for you to earn payment every three months. Say goodbye to financial inadequacy.

Investment in Dividend Stocks Translates to a Sufficient Income in the Retirement Period

When you invest in dividend stock for the long term, you're privileged to have a stable income when you retire. Here is a reason why you should invest in dividend stocks, and do so as soon as possible.

Research by several finance professionals shows that investors who build a dividend stock portfolio for the long term are more likely to acquire many shares when they age. The implication of having many Dividend-paying stocks at an old age or retirement period is that you have more than enough money to cater to your financial problems.

You should invest in dividend-paying stocks because they are futuristic than their counterparts. When you buy dividend-paying stocks, you are confident in your decision, as you know that you are making a financial decision that guarantees financial freedom. Investing in dividend stocks brings you both short-term and long-term rewards.

For instance, a nurse named Jane makes steps towards securing her financial future by investing in dividend stocks by the time she is 40. If her dividend income is $50 at the time, with time, the income grows to $100 and continuously adds up. By the time she is 60, Jane's dividend income would have added up to $20,000 that rolls in equity. So, if you want to be like Jane, or even better, invest in dividend stocks.

Investment in Dividend Stocks Grants You the Privilege to Retain Your Shares and Ownership at the Same Time

Dividend stocks are not like other investment options. Typically, if you invest in a stock that does not pay a dividend, the only way for you to make money out of your shares is by selling them out. The implication of this is that you cannot make a profit and retain ownership of your shares. With ordinary shares, you cannot earn a profit while maintaining your stocks; you have to give in something for something, vis-à-vis.

The fear of losing ownership to gain profit is what pushes many people away from investing. They are incredibly skeptical of any form of investment due to their generalization of stocks. Not all stocks are the same. Dividend stocks, for instance, is significantly different from other types of stocks that do not pay dividends. Naturally, as humans, we are selfish, and we don't love losing out. Thus, we always want to gain. We don't accommodate the fear of making a loss; this is why some investors do not like the idea of selling shares. They are of the notion that selling their stocks in a company will affect them, especially in periods where growth is probable. So, people tend to reject the idea of investing in stocks as they believe earning profit makes them lose their source of income and ownership in a company.

As earlier stated, all stocks are not the same. The shares which prevent dual privilege of ownership and profitability are those that do not pay in dividends. Dividends paying stocks permits you to make money off your shares while still being in control of them. If you invest in dividend stocks, you do not have to fear the relinquishment of your ownership in a company.

With an investment in dividend stocks, you make a profit off your stocks while owning them for the possibility of capital appreciation.

Inflation Has Almost Nothing on Dividend Stocks

During inflation periods, your earnings are affected negatively. Despite the negative effect of inflation, you can keep your passive income safe from the negative impact that inflation hampers on the economy. When you invest in dividends paying stocks, you can WIN (Whip Inflation Now).

If you are a follower of history, then you are likely to remember that the WIN word came about in President Gerald Ford's administration. If you are ignorant about what happened, here is a quick recap. Back in August 1974, President Ford charged Americans to Whip Inflation Now (WIN) as there was a growing rate of inflation in the country then (about 11%). And the WIN strategy proved useful for most Americans as it provided a hedge against inflation.

Investment in dividend stocks protects your investment earnings from inflation; thus, if you are looking forward to ample protection in inflation periods. If you want to smile while others are crying wolf, invest in dividend stocks.

A significant benefit of dividends over most income-generating investments is that they can keep pace with the rate of inflation. Dividend stock prices increase as the general price level in an economy increases. When prices inflate, companies gain more profit. The increased earnings of companies permit them to increase the rates of dividend payments. Consequently, you make more profit as an investor. However, inflation still takes a bite out of your investment income as a modest 3% inflation has the potential to reduce the 7% on your annual earnings to a meager sum of 4%.

Investing in Dividend Stocks Provides a Win-Win Opportunity

Most investment generating options do not allow you to win totally. For instance, you are an investor solely in ordinary shares that do not pay in dividends; you are likely to succeed in only one way. The only way that you can win is if you sell the stock at a high price. Ironically, you suffer a more significant loss as instability is almost synonymous with Wall Street (stock exchange market). There is no surety that share prices will increase to an amount that earns you profit. Even if a while is stable, the stability is often short-lived due to frequent fluctuations of shares value. Therefore, there is a probability that you may lose in two ways when you invest in ordinary shares. You drop in profitability at regular intervals, and more importantly, you lose the ownership of your stocks.

The situation of things is a little bit better when you invest in dividend stocks. While you are subject to the same culture of the instability of Wall Street, you are more secure when you invest in dividends stocks. Unlike other types of shares, dividends provide the win-win option. You have considerably stable ownership of your stocks while making money from it in your possession. If the issuing corporation pays you your dividend check and your stock value increase at the same time, you make terrific money from income and capital appreciation. If you don't want to earn your dividend immediately, you can reinvest it to buy more stocks.

As earlier stated, Wall Street is not all bed of roses. You can equally lose out when you invest in dividend stocks. Investing in dividend stocks does not give you immunity from frequent loss. But you are safer than when you rely only on shares that do not reward in dividends.

Chapter 8 - Growth Investing

Growth investing is often contrasted with value investing as being a completely different style of making money in the markets. The truth is that both approaches overlap with one another. This is going to give you a good introduction to growth investing, as well as clarify how you can capture growth profitably and with as little risk as possible in your portfolio.

Definition

So, what is growth investing anyway, and why is it a good strategy to follow? As the name suggests, the idea here is to capture the growth inherent in a company. The aim is to identify companies that have huge growth prospects for the future and have the earnings and competitive edge to back this up. The focus of growth investing is to capture capital gains.

This is because companies that are growing fast need all the cash, they can get their hands on. Therefore, paying dividends might not be the best option. Thus, investors who place their money in growth stocks are banking on the stock price rising enough so as to make them enough gains in the long run. This sounds like a risky strategy, but it's actually what proper investing is all about.

After all, the aim is to capture the rise in stock price when you invest your money. Growth based strategies simply take this a step further and demand that a company has an excellent competitive edge as well as a fair price valuation. This is where growth investing can be contrasted with value investing. Value investors tend to focus quite a bit on the price of the investment.

Let's say there are two companies A and B. Let's say A is a not so great company that is not going to last more than 10 years from the current date. On the other hand, B is a great company that has excellent growth prospects. Currently, A is selling for a price that is worth around 65% of its value, while B is selling for 95% of its value as an investor might calculate it.

The value investor would typically pick A while the growth investor would pick B. This helps highlight one of the biggest advantages of growth investing. It is designed to be a long-term strategy by its very definition. Companies don't grow overnight and in order to realize all of the benefits of the strategies, you need to stay invested for the long-term.

Let's take a look at some of the other advantages of investing this way.

Great Companies

Growth investing strategies place a huge premium on a company remaining competitive over long periods of time. Over the long run, a company's stock price tracks its growth in earnings. Therefore, in order for the price to grow, the earnings have to grow as well at a good pace. The only way this can happen is if the company has a strong competitive edge in the market and in its industry.

All of the big companies you hear about today were once growth-oriented companies. For example, Apple was prototypical growth stock around 2002-2003. The company was gearing up to release its next generation of products and Steve Jobs' vision for the company had only just begun to be fulfilled. The company had a very strong competitive advantage in that it could charge whatever price it wanted for its products and customers were still willing to pay.

In fact, customers were willing to line up for hours outside Apple stores for the products. Any Apple product release was a major event and soon, their products spawned entire side industries such as accessories for iPods and iPhones. The interesting thing was that at no point in this growth journey was Apple stock cheap by standard metrics.

The company sold for a pretty high multiple compared to its earnings. In 2003 the stock closed at $1.05. Today the stock sells for $267.99. Keep in mind that this is after multiple stock splits. Apple issued a 2 for 1 stock split in 2006 and another 7 for 1 stock split in 2014. This means that real gains are well above the difference in stock prices between then and now.

Is Apple still a growth stock? Probably not. It is the biggest company in the world and it has seemingly exhausted its creative ability when it comes to launching earth-shattering products. This is not a bad thing by itself. It is tough for large companies like Apple to keep innovating and disrupting their industries. It is far more profitable for them to simply maintain their position in the industry and consolidate.

My point is that the rewards of growth investing are massive. Just like Apple, Amazon was once a growth stock. Some might argue that it still is a growth stock. Microsoft was once a growth stock, as was Walmart, IBM, Intel, and so on.

Cutting Edge

Growth investing companies tend to maintain their advantage in the market for long periods of time. This is because the industries they operate in tend to be at the forefront of change. Using Apple as an example, once again, the technology industry has seen a massive change from what it used to be at the turn of the millennium.

Growth investing thus helps you capture not just company growth, but you receive the boost of being invested in an entire industry as well. Thus, it isn't as if just one stock is rising, but an entire group of companies are rising. This tends to fuel even more growth since more investors jump into these stocks. Along with Apple, Google,

Facebook, Amazon, and Netflix have witnessed huge surges in stock price.

Netflix is a good example of how the rise of an entire sector can help a company. Netflix started off as a small-time competitor of Blockbuster's mail-order movie service. However, they soon pivoted to a streaming service back before anyone even knew what 2G was. Many people did not understand the business model, nor did they grasp the enormity of the CEO, Reed Hastings' vision.

Hastings' bet was to take advantage of the rise of tech services and infrastructure over the last few years of the past decade so as to give Netflix a viable platform. Setting aside the fact that the tech industry lived up to its promise, consider a world where tech companies were not generating any buzz and that Silicon Valley wasn't slowly replacing Wall Street as the economic center of America.

The chances of Netflix succeeding in such an environment would have been extremely low. Without the buzz that was reflected in the company from the rise of tech at large, no one would have paid any deep attention to the rise of the company or its business model. As it stands today, Netflix has many competitors, but it still holds a major place in the hearts and minds of people that buy its services.

This just shows that by following growth investing principles, not only will you find one investment, but you'll end up unearthing an entire world of investments and companies that will rise along with it and take their place in the new economy.

Excitement

This one is counterintuitive but stay with me here. A lot of investors find it difficult to stick to their long-term strategies since they tend to be boring. For example, if you invest in individual stocks that pay good dividends, then you're going to find a lot of your money parked in utility stocks. Utility companies aren't exactly setting the world on fire.

They're in highly regulated industries and their prices are capped. They're safe bets and their earnings are extremely predictable. Their stock prices won't decline too much during bear markets, but neither will they rise too much in bull markets. In short, they're the picture-perfect boring stock. Many investors will find it tough to stick to their discipline and stick to these investments.

They'll crave excitement since this is what the overwhelming messaging with regards to the stock market is. They'll hear their friends and neighbors talking about exciting investments and will want some of that action. As a result, they'll end up switching strategies and will not stick to the long-term holdings rule.

Growth investing mitigates this to a large extent since the companies you will end up unearthing are in exciting and cutting-edge industries. Their stock prices will be volatile. Volatility refers to the degree to which the price moves in either direction. Growth stocks' prices tend to jump around a lot and this provides some sense of entertainment.

The downside is that if they move too far to the downside, investors might sell. However, if the companies choices are right, and if you follow the advice in this part, your downside is going to be limited and this makes it unlikely you'll sell. Instead, you'll see the stock doing something every day and this brings its own sense of validation with it.

Therefore, you're much more likely to stick to your strategy and not end up sabotaging yourself by selling too early.

Conclusion

Stock market investment is one of the best ways to protect your hard-earned money. During recession, most of the companies struggled to keep their heads above water, and the majority of the regular citizens started to protect their savings from irreparable loss. Most of the regular stock buyers started to walk away from the share markets, but few people who are intelligent purchased the shares which were at an unbelievable lower price. When the stock value of big companies fall you can purchase the stock at a lower price, and it is the best time to buy shares.

Stock market investment is no more a mystery, thanks to the era of the internet which helps you to set up your account from home and start a modern way of investing in the stock market. In the past, people have to run after the share brokers to know about the value of shares and to have a look at their account details. But these days everything has become transparent, and you can have a view at your account details and the recent prices of the stocks from being at home comfortably.

Well, only one thing is certain, and that is change. Changes are always certain, so does the experienced stock world. It has moved on to cyberspace from the clattered, clumsy stock markets, which looks nonetheless fish markets. The evolution of the Internet is the reason for the revolution in stock markets as well as another trading. It got the easy access feature along with the comfort of operating stocks from one's office or home. The speedy technology acted as a catalyst to break the norms of the stock market. It is no more an alien world for people. Rather, it got unearthed, and the mysteriousness of this trading place just vanished. Now, people are comfortable trading online, and the investors and their investments have increased three-fold. The bulls and bears are no more only confined to the creams rather it has skimmed to the commons.

Being a stock-market investor, you should keep an eye on the market trend and ready to face the downfall at any time as there are risks in this business that are fairly high and severe in some cases.

You should know about the company and the market trends before investing your precious money in the stock market. The company's future goals and aspirations can be very helpful for you to make the right decisions.

At the end of a well-run marathon, fatigue is accompanied by an exhilarating sense of achievement. All the planning, all the obsessing, all the training in all types of weather: it all seems worth it. Not just "worth it," but an invaluable experience that, I believe, makes one a better person.

With a well-run investment plan, you get the same sense of accomplishment. Long-range planning and patience pay off.

College education for your children and a comfortable retirement for you: you have set your goals and achieved them. And, if you invest successfully enough, you may choose to donate some of your profits to charities and causes you support—making you a better person and the world a better place.

Just as importantly, you will be in control of your finances. You will become comfortable with the ups and downs of the market and of individual stocks. You will hold high-quality dividend-paying stocks for the long term. You will know what could go wrong, but you will also know there is a lot that can (and probably will) go right.

Perhaps you never thought you could do it. Now you know you can, so why not give it a shot?

Hopefully, you have found this to be informative, and you have learned a lot about swing trading. Most importantly, I hope that this has helped you to determine whether or not swing trading is something that you would like to do in order to earn profits.

Swing trading can be exciting, fun, and it can also be lucrative. For people who are interested in finance, the markets, and large corporations, swing trading can be a great and fun way to earn a living. It takes time and discipline to become good at swing trading. But if you master it, you can enjoy financial freedom while working from home or practically anywhere as long as you have a computer nearby. Swing trading not only offers the potential of financial reward, but it can also offer you the freedom that is a financially independent life can provide.

I wish everyone a complete success on their journey to make this happen. But we have to be honest and admit that getting there is not necessarily going to be easy. There are going to be mistakes along the way. You may even lose a significant amount of money. One of the traits that a successful trader has to have is you have to be persistent. That includes having the ability of two being able to bounce back from defeats. The main thing when it comes to running into trouble swing trading is that you need to learn from your mistakes. Hopefully, readers will not get involved in trading, have one or two bad trades, and give up. If you get in that situation, go back, study the fundamentals of swing trading, and look at the mistakes you made the call sure trades to go bad. Then dust yourself off and get up and try again.

In the end, though, swing trading may not be for everyone. So do not get depressed if it does not work out for you. Along the way, however, something to consider is applying swing trading in different markets if you find that your first stab at it does not work. One thing that I know was going to happen is a lot of people are going to be interested in swing trading on Forex. For some reason, the currency exchange market holds a lot of appeal for a lot of people. And that is fine as far as it goes. Many people are actually pretty successful on the market. At the same time a lot of people or not, because that is a really touchy market. So, my advice if you decide to start off trading Forex, and it does not work out for you, is that you should not give up on swing trading altogether. Instead, try regrouping and then, even though it is not quite as exciting, try swing-trading stocks instead.

CPSIA information can be obtained
at www.ICGtesting.com
Printed in the USA
LVHW080533280521
688664LV00007B/773